Book Description

So you just saw a picture from your child's recent school trip and noticed them sitting alone, while other children play together. As a parent, your heart races. Are they okay? What can I do? What does my child need?

We know that friendships are beautiful and essential. They teach children to socialize, support one another, and communicate. Children who fail to learn basic social skills run risks of negative experiences later in life.

So what should a parent do?

In *How Parents Can Foster Friendship in Children*, we look at the role friendships play in life. We also offer advice on helping children build relationships with their peers - with some gentle guidance from the parents. We will also examine the relationship between parents and children - what works, and what doesn't.

As the other support network in a child's life, parents teach children how to communicate and empathize in the home. But through this guide, we hope to explore how to translate those skills to any social network outside of the home. We will discuss this important element of parent-child relationships, and how it can be cultivated without power struggles.

In short, you will find everything you need to help your child make friends, to lead responsibly as a good parent, and to enjoy the joys and happiness that come with raising your child.

How Parents Can Foster Friendship in Children

Begin a Meaningful Relationship With Your Child as Both Parent and Friend - Without the Power Struggle

Frank Dixon

professional advice. The content within this book has been derived from various sources. Please consult a licensed professional before attempting any techniques outlined in this book.

By reading this document, the reader agrees that under no circumstances is the author responsible for any losses, direct or indirect, that are incurred as a result of the use of the information contained within this document, including, but not limited to, errors, omissions, or inaccuracies.

Before we begin, I have something special waiting for you. An action-packed 1 page printout with a few quick & easy tips taken from this book that you can start using today to become a better parent right now!

It's my gift to you, free of cost. Think of it as my way of saying thank you to you for purchasing this book.

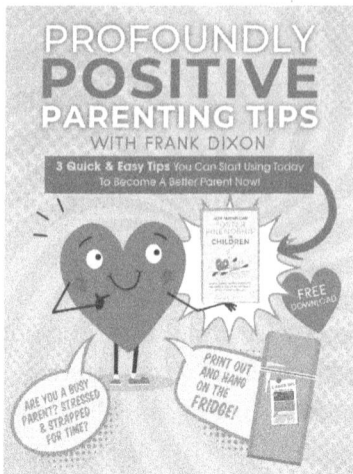

Claim your download of Profoundly Positive Parenting with Frank Dixon by scanning the QR code below and join my mailing list.

Sign up below to grab your free copy, print it out and hang it on the fridge!

Sign Up By Scanning The QR Code With Your Phone's Camera To Be Redirected To A Page To Enter Your Email And Receive INSTANT Access To Your Download

Before we jump in, I'd like to express my gratitude. I know this mustn't be the first book you came across and yet you still decided to give it a read. There are numerous courses and guides you could have picked instead that promise to make you an ideal and well-rounded parent while raising your children to be the best they can be.

But for some reason, mine stood out from the rest and this makes me the happiest person on the planet right now. If you stick with it, I promise this will be a worthwhile read.

In the pages that follow, you're going to learn the best parenting skills so that your child can grow to become the best version of themselves and in doing so experience a meaningful understanding of what it means to be an effective parent.

Notable Quotes About Parenting

*"Children Must Be Taught How To Think,
Not What To Think."*

— Margaret Mead

"It's easier to build strong children than to fix broken men [or women]."

- Frederick Douglass

"Truly great friends are hard to find, difficult to leave, and impossible to forget."

— George Randolf

"Nothing in life is to be feared, it is only to be understood. Now is the time to understand more, so that we may fear less."

— Scientist Marie Curie

Table of Contents

Introduction 1

Chapter 1: Understanding Friendship 3

    The Meaning of Friendship 5

    What Connects Us? 6

    The Qualities of a Good Friend 7

Chapter 2: Essential Friendship Building Skills 11

    Building Blocks of an Everlasting Friendship 11

    Does My Parenting Style
    Impact My Child's Friendships? 16

Chapter 3: How to Make Friends 19

    Befriending at Different Ages 19

        Young Friendships 20

        School-Age Friendships 21

        Teenage Friendships 24

Chapter 4: Friendships in School 27

    How to Help My Child
    Navigate Friendship Issues 28

        Do 29

        Don't 31

Chapter 5: Friendships at Home 33

The Need for Healthy
Friendship Between Parents 34

Should I Be Friends With My Child? 37

A Parent as Friend 37

A Parent as Parent 38

So, Where's the Middle Ground? 39

Chapter 6: Fostering Healthy Bonds 43

Power Struggles in Relationships 44

How to Lead Without a Power Struggle 45

Chapter 7: Friendship FAQs 50

Conclusion 55

References... 57

Introduction

Good friendships in life are a godsend. No matter what age you are, you'll never forget the time spent with friends. The thought takes us back to those carefree days and nights when we used to play outside or share stories in secret under a blanket. The joy they bring into our lives and the colors they add to our palette is truly remarkable.

There are many benefits to early childhood friendships. For many children, their social circles allow them an outlet for their curious mind, beyond the home or classroom. Children learn and grow from each other, much like lion cubs at play. Friendships also help us set and accomplish our goals, whether to complete a project or find extracurriculars. It's always easier for a child to join a sports team if they join with a friend. Friends encourage us and boost our confidence. Looking back, we all know how much easier it was to be social when we had a buddy system.

Equally important, a good friend is always there to pick us up when we fall. A real connection to someone can feel like a port in a storm. With the rapid changes in any child's life, including the significant shift of puberty, a social circle becomes important to make sense of it all. These ideas even have sound academic backing, as studies have shown that friendships help children develop many emotional and social skills, and improve their sense of belonging (Jones et al., 2015).

A child behavior expert, Paul Schwartz, suggests that friendships contribute to the development of skills such as sensitivity towards one another and acceptance of differences in opinions (Schwartz, n.d.). A social circle also enables children to keep pace with age-appropriate behaviors. According to Schwartz, children with smaller circles reported early trouble interacting with peers and depicting emotional stability.

In another research study, scientists also found that friendships can have a positive impact on the academic performances of children (Fletcher et al., 2013). Friends help each other in discouraging deviant behavior, especially those within the same academic program, and often report high self-esteem and advanced coping mechanisms.

In this book, we will explore the importance of long-lasting friendships and help our children form them without hesitation. We will also look at the important relationship between a parent and child, and whether we need to seek "friendship" with our children.

Chapter 1: Understanding Friendship

Author C.S. Lewis (*The Chronicles of Narnia*) once said, "Friendship is born at that moment when one person says to another: "What! You too? I thought I was the only one" (1960). This idea has reflections even in antiquity, as Greek philosopher Plato also spoke on this unique relationship, stating, "Similarity begets friendship" (2013). I think we can all agree that similar interests are often an indicator of close friendships. But that's not always entirely true. How many of us had or still have friends that are complete opposites of ourselves? If we like romantic comedies, they would insist on science fiction. If we want chocolate, they would prefer vanilla. Our interests may not align, but we still consider them good friends.

These relationships are so important to us, so intriguing, that researchers throughout history have always wanted to know how they develop. Was there some hidden motive behind friendship? Were these relationships based on a tit-for-tat, or, "you scratch my back and I scratch yours" approach? Or was there something more abstract to it all?

To solve this puzzle, researchers looked at the animal kingdom for a clue. Animals were believed to have less manipulation in their behaviors, or less ulterior motives - unlike human beings - and thought to be motivated simply by food or mates (Mourier et al., 2012).

In one study, a group of French scientists observed 133 blacktip reef sharks in an attempt to determine if they occupied the same space at the same time, and if they had similar groupings to humans (Mourier et al., 2012). After monitoring their behavior for weeks, these scientists were surprised to note that many sharks indeed preferred the company of specific others and even went out of their way to avoid the rest. These groupings could be considered parallel to human social circles.

In another experiment, researchers asked participants to form a list of ten of their closest friends, and to assign one hundred "points" between them on a scale of closeness (DeScioli & Kurzban, 2009). When one group of participants were told that their answers would be kept confidential, they rated their friends truthfully. However, when another group was told that their results would become public, those participants allocated their points equally among their friends. In the latter group, each friend received around ten points, while in the former, some had gotten twenty while others had just five. The study concluded that friendship heavily affects one's reputation. Humans want to maintain a good reputation among friends, in order to stay connected.

The Meaning of Friendship

While scientists continue to study the factors of friendship, we can run some general conclusions. Friendship is built on trust, intimacy, and esteem between two or more people. It suggests a sense of safety and confidentiality, and acts as a support system. What separates friendship from basic companions or acquaintances are five items:

1. *Interaction.* Friendship is regarded at its core as a dyadic relationship - occurring between two people - and is based on interactions between those people. Those interactions build history, familiarity, and expectations. Meeting those expectations builds trust. Styles of interaction have evolved over the years, but online interactions still develop the familiarity essential to friendship.

2. *Reciprocated Affection.* Friendship is a give-and-take relationship, where both partners are invested in the lives of each other. A unique bond is created through their mutual attraction and respect.

3. *No Legalities.* Unlike other legal relationships, friendship isn't obligatory or legally binding. There is no contract to sign, but simply based on mutual consent. Thus, these bonds can become as strong or as weak as your level of investment.

4. *Egalitarian in Nature.* Both individuals share the same power and voice as the other.

Friendship is democratic. It is thus difficult to maintain friendship between individuals with different power levels - especially if they share a home or work environment.

5. *Shared activities*. Participating in a project or experience together builds companionship. Companionship is a primary foundation of any blooming friendship. It develops when people feel comfortable and valued in each other's company.

These five features are what differentiate friendships from other common relationships. The presence of any, if not all, of these features differentiates a friend from another peer group.

What Connects Us?

It may be shared interests, or it may be a sense of security, but what else can bring us together?

A common feature of friendship and social circles is shared histories. This could mean shared experiences or familiar stories through race, geography, ethnicity, or religion. In this case, a similar background may develop similar understandings and perspectives of the world. Shared histories could also mean some similar experience two individuals have gone through, such as the separation or loss of a parent. It is much easier to talk to someone with the same experiences as you, especially on a difficult or unfamiliar subject.

Two individuals could also share common values. Common values create friendships with less strain, while differing views have an extra stress factor. However, again, differences don't mean the relationship won't work, and in many ways, differences can actually create a valuable learning experience. That shared experience then further strengthens a bond.

Importantly, friendships also tend to develop along lines of equality. There must be equality between both partners for a friendship to succeed in the long-term. If one individual feels that they give without receiving the same compassion and care in return, they may feel slighted, or taken for granted. Both partners need support and encouragement to create value in the relationship. Thus, both partners need to put in equal effort.

The Qualities of a Good Friend

The general qualities of a good friend are familiar to us. They share unique interests and skills. They have a unique personality that blends with ours. We always feel comfortable in their company. But unfortunately, there isn't an exact formula to determine who your friends will be.

We connect with who we communicate with. It can be a neighbor, a classmate, or another family with a similar commute. You could meet in the grocery store, or at the playground. Introductions have no set format. If children are younger, their interactions are more natural, with less learned social anxiety to hold them back. They sit with, learn with, and play with others in an unseeming pattern. Eventually, familiarity forms and bonds are created. For older children, interactions are based on shared experiences and common interests. They may have a project together in art class, or play the same instrument in the school band.

Teenagers are much more complex. At this age, new social dynamics emerge, social pressures offer new expectations, and puberty sends emotions into overdrive. In this overwhelming stage, friends are very important to help navigate these new feelings. They are formed through common experiences, but grasped quickly, and held on to tightly. In this way, it can be difficult for a student in a new school to make friends, as friendships and cliques have been pre-established. But once a real connection is made, it can mean the world to that new student.

In all, the following traits are considered the most admired qualities of a good friend:

1. *Trustworthiness*. Trust is what keeps a relationship bound. When a friend is trustworthy, it means that you can be your true self with them, acting without pretense. You can rely on them to share private experiences, acknowledge feelings, and keep a secret without judgement. True and trustworthy friends offer us a safe space.

2. *Kindness*. A kind friend is considerate and compassionate. They stand with you, comfort you, and help you without expecting anything in return. They are genuinely interested in your life and want you to have the best.

3. *Honesty*. An honest friend doesn't offer fake appreciation. They are straightforward when they need to be, and will tell you when they are confused or disappointed by a choice you make. But they will also gladly tell you when they love and respect your choices. They are invested in your wellbeing.

4. *Unconditional Support*. A genuine friend will support you in a mistake and help you grow from it. Their support may come in different forms, such as emotional support when we feel low or insecure, or practical support when we need to handle a problem. They will always have your back.

5. *Acceptance*. We all carry flaws and imperfections. A true friend will accept those of us, without trying to mold us into someone else. Without envy or condescension, an accepting friend will let you exist as you are.

6. *Emotional Availability*. We should all be able to feel wanted, heard, and seen. An available friend knows how to pull us out of our miseries and look at the bright side. They pop over when we feel lonely, and don't leave until they've boosted our mood. Always just a call or text away.

7. *Comfort.* A friend should make us feel safe, protected, and covered. When we are close friends with someone, there is no reluctance when it comes to asking for favors. With a close friend, it doesn't feel like putting your partner in a bad position. We trust that they really need the favor, and they trust us to take care of it. Every bond strengthens when ideas are heard and accepted.

8. *Forgiveness.* A forgiving friend will not press you if you fall short in your responsibilities. They don't hold grudges, they listen to reason, and they are willing to sort things out. They trust you to learn and give you space to grow

Chapter 2: Essential Friendship Building Skills

As friendship is such an important part of our lives, contributing in part to our very personalities, how do we, as parents of toddlers and adolescents, help our children make friends? It can be difficult to accept that our role is limited. Ultimately, a child needs to make these decisions on their own, and so the best a parent can do is teach them the right skills. Many of these skills are straightforward, focusing on kindness, proper conversation, inclusion, and active listening. Those skills are helpful because they make those first few interactions less stressful. That old adage rings true - first impressions are hard to break. It will always be harder later to nudge in and join a conversation that has already started. To establish friendships, social skills are important, helping to make introductions more natural and less forced. With these skills in their pocket, your child will be best prepared for a future of friendship.

Building Blocks of an Everlasting Friendship

Social skills include interpersonal skills, such as active listening, cooperation, collaborative play, patience, and empathy. These are important to teach early on as they set the pace for improved relationships over a lifetime. Children who develop emotional intelligence, kindness, generosity, and empathy are likely to do well in academics and lead happier lives than those who lack these essential skills. Happier lives mean success, reduced stress, and fulfilled goals. As parents we need to do our best to encourage our children to form strong bonds and have someone to share ideas and thoughts with. Once these connections are made they create an intertwined growth - stronger together than apart.

Communication Skills

Friendship, and any other relationship, relies on communication. Friendship is very difficult to sustain between friends without talking to each other. Without similar interests or values, friends may find it difficult to share with one another, and drift apart. At times, conflicting values can stimulate good conversation between friends, but those conversations require careful attention and balance. Therefore, good communication skills are essential for every child. They must know how to start, carry on, and end a conversation when appropriate. They must develop a delicate social filter to speak openly, but carefully, to make others feel interested, but not uncomfortable. They must also be willing to share when the conversation requires it, and listen in turn.

Listening Skills

Listening skills are the hidden star of good conversation. It is not enough to have something to say, but rather, to have the right thing to say. It is not talking for the sake of filling a silence. From an early age, children are naturally excellent listeners, soaking up the world around them and reacting with deep empathy. As they are socialized into conversation, they tend to lose this skill as they try to make an impact on their environments. Parents, in turn, need to reinforce these active listening skills with their developing children. An active listener is one who doesn't just react, but responds empathetically. Teach your children to focus not just on the verbal cues, but also on non-verbal cues like a friend's body language, facial expressions, and tone of voice. Focus on what is being said without distractions, or getting lost in their thoughts. And importantly, they must read these cues for the right time to respond. For example, when the moment requires it, or their partner has said their piece. Often, a friend just needs to let it out and be heard. Try not to offer unsolicited advice or try to fix things unless asked to.

Fair Play Skills

Younger children, in particular, have a hard time sharing and following fair play. Playing is really only fun when both players are fair. Rules need to be softly reinforced to dissuade cheating. A bad experience at playtime does not lend itself to a lasting bond of friendship. Naturally, there will be some drama in encouraging balanced play time, but better the drama be on you as a disciplinarian, than more personal and amongst the children themselves.

Eventually, they will learn to expect to share, and the drama will subside.

Empathy

We all must be considerate of the feelings of others. But as a less tangible skill, this can be difficult to teach. Simply encourage your children to look for and recognize the feelings of others. Don't disregard them as if they aren't important. Treat other individuals like icebergs and look for the other 90% hidden below the surface. Body language lends context to conversation, so seek out these clues. Your child is a natural empath when it's born, feeding on the emotions of the mother and father. So feed these empathy abilities and let them blossom - don't stifle them so soon in the difficulties of a daily schedule. Trust in yourself and be patient. If done correctly, your child should come to accept the feelings of others, without judgment. Again, that feeling of being seen and heard can be an incredibly powerful tool to create lasting friendships.

Patience

We all need to practice this skill, not just children. So do your best as you teach your child, and be patient even with yourself. This skill applies across any context, whether in conversation or at play. Give others a chance when they are speaking, without interrupting. Look out for others, and understand that we will all have a turn when the moment is right.

Accepting Wins and Losses

Life isn't fair and games certainly aren't either. Someone has to lose in order for someone to win. Whether your child wins or loses, they should know how to accept it graciously. It is difficult to stay friends with an ungracious loser or a gloating winner. The same rules of fair play apply here. Teach your children to express decently and with grace. Encourage them to win or lose without excuses or grudges. Games are practice for real world encounters, so be sure to play them respectfully.

Acceptance Skills

Children must be taught to accept others as they are. They shouldn't discriminate against someone based on their height, weight, or other physical features. They shouldn't belittle others from a different background or experience. They mustn't bully or fight with people who don't share the same opinions as them. They should instead appreciate and accept everyone's unique qualities and differences. In doing so, the doors of friendship open more frequently.

Conflict Resolution

In any relationship, conflicts, arguments, and differences of opinions are bound to occur. Your child may insist on playing a certain game indoors while their friend wishes to ride bikes outside in the sun. As friends, they must be able to compromise, whichever form it takes to them. Encourage your children not to frame conflicts as win-or-lose encounters. There will always be a third, fourth, or fifth option. Real friends will look for these other options. Empathy is a great skill here, so that we can see from our friend's perspective. Teach them to put aside their personal gains and find ways in which they can gain together as partners.

Does My Parenting Style Impact My Child's Friendships?

As parents, we want our kids to have the right friends. People who lift them, inspire them, and motivate them to pursue their goals in life. We might want to help them first and be there for them before others, but as children grow older, they stop relying on us and rely more on their friends. It can be a painful truth that friends may understand each other better than a parent-child relationship can. The unconditional love of a parent is strongest above all, but it can also be healthy for a child to have multiple support systems.

We often assume that parenting is hard. However, we occasionally forget how hard it can be for a child too. They go through a lot, and very quickly. It takes real commitment to stay friends with someone. Having someone to hang out with at school, in college, or at the office is encouraging. But everyone is raised in a different household, and under a different parenting style. Children emerge from our homes, each uniquely affected by that parenting style, and use our past-down knowledge to build their friendships. Interestingly, new research suggests that parents can be one of the many reasons why some kids struggle with making friends at school or in college.

Published in Science Daily, a recent joint study from the University of Jyvaskyla and Florida Atlantic University suggested that negative parenting strategies, which lower a child's self-esteem, ultimately affects the formation of friendships in their lives (Dickson et al., 2018). Collecting data from 1,523 children in grades one to six, the study analyzed the characteristics of the parents and their parenting style, as well as the friendships of their children. The collaborative team from both universities identified three important elements of parenting when it comes to forming relationships:

1. The degree to which warmth and affection was shown to the child
2. Behavioral control (using strict rules and regulations)
3. Psychological control (using guilt and shaming to impact behavior)

The researchers further suggested that children from households where parents exerted psychological control were most likely to have friendships dissolve later in life. Those children reported loss trust, poor self-esteem, and a lack of social skills; including poor communication and confidence in their abilities to form strong relationships.

As parents, if we fail to teach the basic skills of friendship, and instead become highly demanding and unappreciative parents, we can directly impact the development of our children's relationships.

Chapter 3: How to Make Friends

As a parent, there is much we can do to help our kids establish long-term friendships. We encourage them to say hi to someone new, or to share a toy when they are still young. We play a key role in helping them make those first impressions. However, friendship looks quite different when kids grow older. Parents play a smaller role in their child's social life as they develop a mind of their own and a drive for self-determination. Guidance and monitoring are, however, still the duties of every parent. Just because they have brought someone home from school one day, doesn't mean that they are the best choice for your child. As we discussed in chapter one, not everyone carries the best qualities of friendship, or has your child's goodwill in mind.

In this chapter, we will discuss the role played by parents in fostering friendships at different ages.

Befriending at Different Ages

To help keep our children safe, we need to cultivate good, inspiring, and trustworthy friends around them. The last thing you want is for your child to have their heart broken by a friend who didn't respect them. Not only that, but it is also our job to ensure that the activities among friends are age-appropriate and safe. Negative influences surround us, and a child needs to learn critical awareness and media literacy to successfully navigate their environment. That teaching role still falls upon the parents. It will always be awkward to have "The Talk", but the parent is the most important resource for a child, and needs to offer that lifeline - even if the child doesn't accept it at first. Let your children know you are always ready to talk if they are, but don't push them. Open communication and active listening skills are skills that can help parents too. It allows them to stay involved in their child's life, without lying or secrecy on either end.

So remember to consider your options carefully, and while you can't always select the friends for your child - you can certainly push them in the right direction.

Young Friendships

Kindergarten friends are often made by instinct. For instance, they may want to sit with someone special, or share their toys only with another. As parents, your role here is to be present to ensure they do so safely. You will want to display positive play relationships, and responsible behaviors. For parents, it helps to notice the strengths and weaknesses of their kid, and encourage growth in both areas - but give them space to develop. If you have a particularly shy kid, you can always pop in to check that they feel comfortable, but let them discover their own limits.

Young children are especially great empaths, so use this opportunity to have them check in with their emotions. Help them safely experience hurt, pain, or sadness - and what each means. Help them discover these emotions as displayed by others. Develop their empathy to encourage these skills later in life. Talk to them about keeping calm and not getting frustrated.

School-Age Friendships

School-going years are a fertile time to build friendships. School friends often become life-long friends, and those long-term friends offer a unique perspective to keep you in check as you grow and change. But children are choosier in school. They need time to find similar interests and see if the other can be trusted with their secrets or not. New responsibilities have also entered the child's life. This is a great opportunity to connect with others by sharing those responsibilities, such as studying together for a test. They are also meeting more types of people than ever before, and discovering more about themselves.

As a parent, your role from this point on is that of a coach more than a playmate. You are still in charge, but relegated to the sidelines. But you also provide more direction than ever as they face their intimidating new world. Therefore, continue to emphasize and build their social skills. If your child is shy, teach them coping strategies for peer conflict. If your child is temperamental, teach alternate expressions than anger. Above all, encourage taking a moment to slow down and give others a chance to be their friend, without letting negative thinking overpower them. After all, every other child is in the same place - they're nervous and want to make friends too!

When your child brings a friend home, be welcoming. Go through the rules in the house quickly before leaving them to enjoy themselves. Your child should be a good host in their own home, as well as a good guest in another's. Talk to them about being respectful and asking permission. Teach them to be polite, humble, and accepting.

Get involved one way or the other in your child's life when they are at school. This will allow you to keep an eye on them, but more importantly, provide you with context to their life. For instance, you can join a club event, volunteer to help with fundraising, or join a school sports club. But know your boundaries and don't embarrass anyone. If you notice that they aren't happy about the involvement and look for ways to avoid meeting you when you visit their school, take a step back and don't push them. Be present but tone down the visits.

If the thought of your children having access to a phone scares you, then delay giving them one, and explain to them why. Develop the necessary social literacy skills before you give in. But always remember that a significant amount of communication and bonding takes place online, and this too can be a good opportunity to develop friendships - if done safely and carefully. If you aren't sure about the usage, it is best to put it off until necessary. Consider also making a rule to not have a pin code, but don't snoop without permission - this could severely damage any relationship - especially a parent-child relationship.

Eventually, your child may find a best friend. They will do everything together, and they will become inseparable. As a parent, the first thing to do is get to know the family of your child's friend. This will make the relationship smoother, as both the parents will be encouraging the strong bond that has been, or is in the process of forming. Be sure to check in with your child frequently to see how they feel about the relationship. These feelings can be intense, and if bent out of shape, can be damaging to emotional growth.

Use this as an opportunity to continue discussions of empathy and the importance of healthy communication. Advise them on the many emotions they are going to experience when things get patchy or rough between them and their friend. Encourage them to see the bigger picture for any change in a friends' behavior, before they accuse them of being a bad friend. If there is trouble, and it is safe, encourage them to stick with their friend - they could probably use someone to talk to. This is the moment when listening skills come in handy.

Teenage Friendships

This is the most difficult phase to navigate for both parents and their kids. They are going through so many hormonal transitions, and academics have become increasingly more important - ramping up the pressure even further. It can take a toll on their mental and emotional health. Sadly, this is also the age when distance between parents and children grows wider. Children will inevitably push back against the involvement of parents in their lives. They prefer privacy and are rather choosy about what they share with their parents. At this moment of your own evolving relationship with your child, it can be a difficult time to fully help them develop their other relationships. But be patient with yourself and stick with it - there is light around the corner.

At this age, negative influences start to enter your child's life. Drugs, parties, and sexual experimentation will be considered, but not necessarily experienced. This is the moment where trust between a parent and child needs to be stronger than ever. Instead of dwelling on the bad, try to focus on the good. If you dwell on the negative possibilities, you will create nothing but stress for yourself and your child. Inculcate them with positive experiences. Ensure that their health is your number one priority. Ensure that they are taking care of themselves and their hygiene. Talk to them about the importance of being safe. Teach them about responsibility and how losing control can impact their future. Sit them down and have a chat about intercourse and how to navigate with precaution. But then do your very best to take a step back and let them discover for themselves. Be their safety net, but don't hover and make them want to escape you. If you've taught them to the best of your ability, and shared all the information you have, they should be okay. You turned out okay after all, didn't you? Have some faith in them, and in yourself.

Give them space, but don't leave them hanging. Their body is changing and their moods are swinging wildly with new hormones and social pressures. Talk to them about these changes so they understand them. In fact, this would be a great moment to encourage them to talk to their friends, who are probably experiencing the same things. Allow the friends to be each other's support system, and take a small step back.

As kids are at the brink of becoming teenagers, their preferences may change in a week. For instance, someone who loved to play with dolls may one day want to throw them all away. Someone who loved to read books might be interested in some game time. All these moments will affect your child too. But when preferences change, so do friendships. Maybe the reason your child and their best friend hung out all the time was that they loved to gossip and do things together. But what if a boyfriend/girlfriend has taken their place? They are bound to feel lonely and taken for granted. So help them see through this and be a rock for them in this moment. Help them navigate their feelings as only a parent can.

Teach them to stand up for themselves if they feel they are being taken advantage of by anybody. They shouldn't have to feel neglected or make up for someone else's shortcomings. Some relationships are not worth keeping or fighting for. Both sides need to be invested. Encourage them to talk it out with a friend or former friend to resolve amicably. Strangely, sometimes you have to walk away in order to be someone's best friend in the moment.

Chapter 4: Friendships in School

School-age children need friends for healthy mental and emotional development. Be it heartbreaks or laughter during the time spent together, they learn many social skills just by being together. Kids who are unable to learn these skills at a young age will face difficulty later in life as they try to adapt. Friendship is more than just having a partner in crime, or a playmate. Friendship teaches children how to communicate better, to resolve conflicts, and to cooperate.

As they work and play together, young children become more able to control their emotions and express them with precision. They also learn to take note of the emotions of others and feel what they are feeling. Friendship also teaches them good negotiation skills, as well as how to cope with challenges. It improves their overall perspective about life because they feel looked after and valued. This also improves their attitude and the way they approach opportunities. Good friends even inspire their counterparts to do better in school. They can help each other problem-solve, study together, and healthily discuss things.

A healthy friendship also improves our self-esteem by providing support to think outside of the box and to give our best shot at everything. Teenagers especially can benefit from a support network of friends. Having one or more trustworthy and uplifting friends can help form a network to pull everyone through health issues like depression, anxiety, eating disorders, and lack of confidence - all by working together.

However, you shouldn't expect a drama-free transition into teenage years and a teenage network of friends. As any child enters their teen years, the drama will be unavoidable as anxiety brings emotions to the forefront. There will be confusion, sexual partners, and priorities changing. When that happens, it is also a parent's role to help them navigate their way through those changes. But most importantly, parents need to know how to get involved - without being too involved!

How to Help My Child Navigate Friendship Issues

So Natalie told Chrissy what I specifically told her not to. I kept her secret about that incident in the bathroom last week. Then why did she have to humiliate me like that in front of the whole science lab?

Sound familiar? If not - it may soon. Despite all your best intentions, and every effort to teach good communication skills, teenagers will eventually learn to speak rather abstractly and obscure the details. They may get offended over what seem to you like little things, but to them are the most important things in the world. And you need to be able to accept this when the time comes. Often the little things are small representations of a much larger problem, so don't brush them away so easily. Patience is key, just trust that your child will open up to you, their trusted source, when they are ready.

Sometimes, it isn't your child causing the scene but rather mutual friends, leaving your child confused and alone. If there are three best friends and two of them decide to have a fight and not talk to one another, the third friend gets punished in that contract for no reason. They may even be pressured into taking a side, and feel they have to prove their friendship to both others individually.

Social drama is common among adolescents. As a parent, if you notice that it is affecting the mental health of your child, you should be concerned. Sometimes, without you realizing, your child may be in a bullied position, simply for trying to prove their loyalty to another.

Therefore, to understand the role you have to play in all this, we have prepared a list of Do's and Don'ts:

Do

1. *Lend Your Ear*. The first thing you need to do to help your child navigate through social drama is to listen. If they come to you with a problem, hear them attentively and ask them

if they would like to discuss the possible solutions or just vent. Pay attention to their non-verbal cues and reciprocate the same to let them know you understand them.

2. *Probe.* As soon as they are done talking, ask them open-ended questions about how they think you can help them. Ask them about their opinions, views, and feelings on the event to know what they went through.

3. *Show Empathy.* Empathizing with them is another way to create that safe space for your child to be more expressive. When they sense that you are genuinely concerned and eager to help, they will feel much better.

4. *Brainstorm Solutions Together.* Now that you two are on the same page, the next sensible step is to work together as partners to look for possible solutions. Even if you know what they should do, don't enforce it. Let them come to the conclusion themselves to reinforce their self-esteem and build confidence.

5. *Ask them about it later.* Once you have helped them find a solution, always follow-up on how things went after they implemented the solution. Don't let it alone so soon - new developments always tend to hamper progress.

Don't

1. *(Don't) Try to fix it.* Being an adult and having experienced something similar in your childhood, it is natural to want to fix things for your child. But always keep in mind that if you do this job for them, you are taking away their chance to be an independent thinker. You want them to be brave and smart about handling their own affairs. Eventually, they will have to rely solely on their own judgement - so help them develop it while you can, and bestow as much problem-solving wisdom as you can.

2. *(Don't) Ask them to change.* Just because a problem is difficult to solve, doesn't mean we should get rid of it. Letting something go unsolved is not a solution - rather, it exacerbates the problem. Therefore, avoid suggesting something as drastic as this and let them work things out in their mind. You need to hold on to the trust you have as a parent, and if you become one of the other voices asking them to change - you risk losing that trust. Believe in them as they are.

3. *(Don't) Be biased.* While telling you what happened, your child may have represented themselves as the victim, and that won't always be the case. Sometimes, they are the ones who started the drama and now want sympathy when their friends turned them down. So don't treat them like a victim if you

know they are at fault. Instead, use this opportunity to show them the mirror and talk about the repercussions their actions had. Trust in their words, but try to ask the right questions to eke the truth out.

4. *(Don't) Allow bullying.* If you think that the actions of your child make them a bully towards other kids, don't hold back from pointing it out. Encourage them as you used to, to see things from the point of view of others. Use it as a lesson in empathy. Subtly remind them how they would have felt if they were at the receiving end of the bullying. Encourage them to apologize and make amends with those they have hurt and teach them that there is no shame in doing so. Bullying stunts the growth of not only your own child - but any other affected child. Don't allow it, and we can all grow together.

Chapter 5: Friendships at Home

Our very first relationships are with our parents. Our first memory is of them smiling at us with tears of joy in their eyes. We remember how they couldn't hold back their excitement when we took our first steps. We remember how proud they had been when we pronounced our first words. And then we made them even more proud by turning out to be well-behaved, obedient, and successful - most of the time. It may be true that we don't remember these experiences exactly, but our parents definitely do. And we surely remember these with our own kids.

Healthy relationships at home between parents and children is what lays the foundation of a happy home. Without a nourishing relationship it can feel like living in a home without walls. Our relationships provide the structure that keeps us safe. Households where parents are violent, emotionally or physically, risk injuring their own children in the same way. Patterns in parents may beget the same patterns in their children. And so be sure to set the right patterns with your children. Use this unconscious mimicry to your advantage and role model strong choices for your kids. The greater your role modelling, the greater your chances of your children discovering a happy and fulfilled life.

In this chapter, we will look at the role good and bad in-home relationships play on the upbringing of a child. And most importantly, we will investigate the age old question: Should I try to be a friend to my child?

The Need for Healthy Friendship Between Parents

Parents play an important role in the development of social skills in children. They are the ones who teach them to interact with others successfully. One of the most important qualities they teach children is how to build respectful relationships based on love, acceptance, and trust. And since the very first relationship children create is with their parents, how they view that relationship can say a lot about the kind of relationships they will seek in life. For instance, if a parent is highly critical and unloving, the child will assume that that's how relationships are supposed to be. So they will allow others to hurt them and they themselves will criticize others - because it has been normalized. Children who have been raised in homes where domestic violence was a norm, run a greater risk of repeating that cycle and reacting with the same anger and frustration towards their own partners. If you witness abuse between your parents - that behavior becomes normalized.

It is always wise to avoid fighting and conflict in the home. If an argument escalates, as they tend to do, more than anything you need to be sure that your child is not caught in the crossfire. It can be difficult to schedule a conflict, but you need to gather control of your emotions for the good of your child. If a child witnesses a conflict, do your best - together, if you can - to explain the cause and the solution to that conflict. Help them understand positive conflict resolution to try and normalize that behavior. It is very easy to lose the trust of a child through conflict, so be sure to control it where you can. That trust will be helpful later in the difficult teenage years.

Conflict at home always carries the risk of seeping into other areas of your child's life. As conflict breeds anxiety and uncertainty, your child may develop these traits. At school, these traits may come out during an exam, or an important academic moment, and potentially damage their advancement or progress. They may not be bullied at school, or study in an anxious classroom - but that conflict at home has now bled into their academics.

Children may also resort back to behaviors and habits they used to have when they were younger. For instance, if the child had a habit of wetting their bed or sleepwalking, conflict and an anxious household could trigger this again. They may also be scared easily, have poor sleep, and hide or stutter words.

It can be difficult to broach this subject with your child. Especially when it comes to personal issues, or big picture concerns they may not be ready to deal with yet. But if you don't communicate with your child, they may begin to blame themselves for what goes on in the house. This internal blame will not only affect their mental peace, but again, also reflect on their academics. They may isolate themselves, break up with their friends, or indulge in risky behaviors to overcome the guilt and confusion.

Teenagers are at a special risk to find other negative ways to deal with conflict in the home. They are more active, self-determined, and able to navigate the outside world. They also have a greater network of friends and acquaintances to reach out to - for better or for worse. Teenagers may skip school, get in trouble with the law, hurt others, or get involved in unsafe or unprotected activities. They may also bully others to feel good about themselves if they're upset, which only feeds the cycle of violence. It is more imperative than ever to communicate honestly with your children when they are teenagers to avoid these lashings out.

Statistical data suggests that in the United States, approximately 15 million children have witnessed at least one incidence of violence in their homes (McDonald et al., 2006). That is 15 million potential new cycles of violence. Of course, it is absolutely not a guarantee - and wrong to suggest a direct link - but may still increase the risk of violence later on in a child's life. When behavior is normalized, it runs this risk. According to another study, girls who have witnessed abuse at home by their father towards their mother are six times more likely to be abused than girls raised in non-abusive families (Monnat & Chandler, 2015). The same study also highlights that boys who have seen their fathers abuse their mothers are ten times more likely to abuse their partners. Abuse should never be tolerated in your household - point of fact.

Should I Be Friends With My Child?

Now that we have established the importance of healthy relationships and the impact any guiding relationship can leave on children, it brings us to the most pressing question: can a parent and child be friends? Or perhaps a better question would be - *should* a parent and child be friends?

A Parent as Friend

Some will argue that this school of thought is indeed the ideal way to parent. On paper, it can seem more casual, comforting, and less suffocating. Many believe that it allows their kids to be more expressive and honest with them, and thus prevent secrecy and dishonesty. Additionally, some believe that it brings them closer to their child, and promotes stability and harmony.

But this is not always the case. A significant flaw outweighs most of those benefits: too much freedom. Although it is healthy for your child to feel free in their actions, limitations aren't a strict negative. Limitations can often be constructive - and coming from a parent, often are. Without the moral guidelines, the role modelling, or the discipline, children can land themselves in hot water. When parents allow excess freedom to their kids, they may start to push the limits. They start to believe that they can get away with anything and don't always make the right choices. If this is the case, a "friendly" parent is not always able to push back or provide wise guidance. Their status has been diminished in the relationship, to just another member of the friend network.

A Parent as Parent

A similar criticism can indeed be levied against parents who restrict freedom *too* much, and who "parent" too heavily. This can be a stifling style of parenting that almost encourages rebellion. So there is a fine balance in this. But the need for a trusted source, a level of responsibility, and the odd bit of discipline often makes traditional parenting a more valued resource than "friendly" parenting.

Many believe that strict parenting is the best way to instill good values and morals. Without this strong guidance, they worry that children can grow wild and rebellious. The thought is that too much freedom is exploitable. Many also think that strict boundaries and parameters for acceptable and unacceptable behaviors speak for themselves, and there is no need to argue about them.

However, this isn't a perfect model either. Not allowing argument or constructive discussion about boundaries doesn't ensure that these rules will be followed. And heavy discipline upon breaking these rules doesn't ensure they will be understood. Without proper reasoning, and an explanation for these boundaries, they can be misconstrued as suffocating. If the boundaries are there to help ensure the safety of your child - try to explain that to them. Help them understand why the fence was erected here, and what lies on the other side. Otherwise, the child is quite likely to vault the fence and find out on their own.

So, Where's the Middle Ground?

If it's not being their friend, and not a disciplinarian, then what is it? Where's the compromise between authority and leniency? How do we provide freedom within a structure, or boundaries within independence?. In order to establish peace and harmony, a strong approach to parenting is to become a mentor figure.

Being a mentor means you have an interest in your child's life, but don't dictate it. You can play with them, but don't become too fixated on doing things for them. You maintain some form of control over their activities but don't hover over them like a helicopter. You are soft but not too soft. You are strict but not too strict. You are there when they need you but not a complete pushover. Ideally, you should be ready to step in when they need you and be prepared to let them live when they don't.

The key is to not overstep at either of the roles. A mentor is together a coach, guide, and teacher. You can provide guidance, but let them solve their own problems. The hardest part is you have to step aside sometimes and let them be hurt - safely - so they can learn from the experience. In the same way, you have to let them enjoy their life, and love life, in order to learn from those positive experiences as well. You can share in these feelings too, and talk about them. When you feel scared, or anxious, check in with your child. But always stay a step behind them, so that if they fall, you can pick them up and tell them that everything will be alright.

Structure and Discipline

No matter what age, all children need some level of discipline and structure in their lives. Structure provides boundaries to test, and charts the world they can explore. Without discipline, they may act rashly, learn consequences another way, and suffer from anxiety and stress. Building strong social skills and giving them directions on how to lead a successful life is only possible when they see you as the one in control, and they respect your position. Having structure allows them to know what is expected of them and what to expect in return. When they have strong self-control, they feel comfortable facing challenges and grabbing opportunities. When a household is unpredictable and values are inconsistent, this structure is difficult to maintain. A mentor-figure parent needs to be able to balance their role in the house carefully to cultivate this environment.

Younger children aren't developmentally and emotionally able to know their boundaries. This can lead to poor decision making and blaming others for their mistakes. When parents are friends instead of a mentor, there is no strong hand to guide them in the right direction and help them cope with the challenges of growing up.

Rules and Boundaries

Some parents only have a single goal in mind when raising children: please them. Although a positive strategy, it doesn't prepare children for the real world when they go out and discover that life isn't a bed of roses. When parents intentionally decide against setting rules and regulations because they assume it would upset their child or stop them from achieving greatness, they are wrong. It really only leads to disappointment and failure.

The reason children need boundaries is that they will instinctively test their surroundings until they brush up against them. Watch a young child crawl - they will continue until they brush up against the edge of their world. Those boundaries need to be set safely so they can be found and understood before crawling into the riskier territory beyond. An interesting case is that too many or too few boundaries can both lead to insecurity and anxiety. Both cases stem from not understanding the environment properly. Without boundaries, the world can be too vast and overwhelming. With too strict boundaries - the world can become small and stifling.

Dependency

When a parent becomes a friend, rather than a mentor-figure, kids start to look up to them for everything. As a "friend," you always have the answers, but now you have become the answer for everything. It is always recommended to keep a healthy separation between the parent and the child. This separation prepares a child for their eventual independence. When parents become friends, and do everything together, it can become harder for the child to imagine a life without them. They may also fail to develop a strong personality and an identity of their own. As a result, they may forever stay in the nest and not function well as an adult. If they do move out and build a romantic relationship, they will have the same expectations from their partner as they had from their parents. That can be a hard role to fill, and unjust to the partner - leading to an imbalanced relationship.

Chapter 6: Fostering Healthy Bonds

Have there been days when you constantly fight with your child? Do you seem to have opposite opinions about everything, like what to order for dinner or what to wear to a family gathering? The disagreements always end, but they still leave behind negative energy – the type that overwhelms us from time to time. It can be hard to get past it and move one. Often, kids just want to be right. As they self-determine, they want to select the answers for once. They want to do things their way and not the way their parents expect them to. The difficulty as a parent is to let them be "right" once in a while, even if you know how it will end up. In your lived wisdom, you need to take a backseat to their youthful drive, and avoid the dangerous condescension that can come with good advice. Without this give-and-take, relationships can become sour. Every time there is a discussion, it ends with another argument and everything falls apart once again. If you have dealt with this behavior lately, you may be stuck in a power struggle.

In this chapter, we come to understand what power struggles are, their impact on the relationship between a parent and a child, and how parents can avoid them.

Power Struggles in Relationships

Imagine this: you told your teenage daughter to clean her room two days ago. It still is in the same condition – if not worse. If you have guests visiting today and are too busy to go upstairs and set it for them. You feel hurt that they didn't adhere to your request. It is difficult to turn this experience into a learning moment, as the consequences will mostly come back on you as the host.

On the other side, your daughter is holding a grudge against you because you grounded her over something you deemed insignificant, which really was everything to her. Her friends went to a party without her and now she is anxious to be excluded from her social circle. She blames you for purposely punishing her so that she would miss the party. She wants to get back at you and show you her independence through protest.

Now both of you are angry at each other, but not ready to talk it out. You two are just waiting for the other to give in and apologize. To make matters worse, you have guests over and have to perform as host for them, without being your real self with your daughter.

This is a power struggle. Power struggles can be about any and everything, no matter how big or small. They usually come with one distinct feature: an ultimatum. An ultimatum could be something as simple as demanding an apology. Ultimatums carry too much pressure, so just don't set them. If you stand by them, you risk dying on your sword for something that could be worked out in a much more effective way. Especially when coupled with negative thoughts, they can only breed discontent, and make things worse.

Power struggles, in any relationship, can be highly toxic. You may recognize them best in the workplace, when there is intense competition or status-shifting among employees. The same takes place inside a household. They are known to bring out the worst in everyone involved, and set roots of bitterness. With children, they often play out through public tantrums, manipulation, and self-doubt. They have an uncanny ability to play a parent against their public image - piercing the veil of social expectations. These reactions often lead to resentment, hatred, and prolonged suffering for both parties. They need to be dealt with from the beginning, stopping conflict from brewing before it begins.

How to Lead Without a Power Struggle

Another scenario to consider. Your child is taking all the time in the world to get dressed and get out of the door. You're already late for work and keep shouting their name to come out. In doing so, you get more frustrated, and they get the secret joy of rebellion. The morning is already ruined for both of you, and once in the car, you avoid talking to each other completely. A question is brought up, and your tone is filled with sarcasm and accusations. Your child reacts accordingly, and you find yourself in another power struggle. Below are some tips to deal with a tense situation effectively, ensuring that your parent-child relationship stays strong. Remember, sometimes you have to take a step back and lose a little ground, in order for a true parenting win.

1. *Let them have the last word.* You might think this is odd and it may be difficult to do. However, it can benefit your relationship greatly. If your child says something negative, don't react. Don't stoke the fire. Be the role model and mentor you need to be, and let it go. Model the behavior you hope to see in them. Set your dignity aside for just a moment. You'll get it back soon - you're the provider and they depend on you. They know this, but a moment can get heated. Once your child lets an insult out of their system and fails to see a charged response, they will cut it out themselves. But set your own boundaries - when enough's enough - you let them know.

2. *Validate their feelings.* When you are in the middle of a power struggle with your child, let them pour their heart out. Listen with compassion without interrupting them. Once they are done, let them know that you have heard them loud and clear, and that you understand why they feel that way. When a

child feels listened to and validated, it helps them be more expressive and calm the next time around. The world can seem like it ignores them sometimes, so don't ignore them as well.

3. *Give them a reason.* Often, children disobey and start a power struggle because they don't have a compelling reason to obey you. They must know why they should do as they are told, and what the consequences are - positive or negative. Give them a choice and let them pick their own consequences. For example, "if you get ready sooner, we will have more time together, more time with your friends, and we will be at each other's throats much less."

4. *Offer a choice.* This is another way of letting them decide for themselves. If the power struggle is happening over homework and the kid tells you how much they hate you when you make them do it, offer them a constructive choice. Again, the world doesn't offer them much choice generally - so give them a bit of agency here in the household to make their own decisions.

5. *Reframe their imagination.* Another tip that works well is a reframing strategy. If your child can't stand still for very long when asked - reframe the question. Ask them to play a soldier, or a different non-military role, and watch them snap to attention. If parents reframe orders in ways that interest children, power struggles can be avoided.

6. *Build your relationship early.* The best way to prevent power struggles is by knowing your child's interests and spending time with them to develop these. If you share interests, the rebellion phase will be less natural. This also serves as a great time to bond. Consider it an investment in their later years. When they turn 25, they will thank you for your investment. That's a long time coming, but it will set them up for life - trust in that.

7. *Be compassionate.* Role model the behaviors you wish to see. Say your own please and thank yous. A child will mimic the role models in their life through instinct. Add to that a kind and warm tone and you are already halfway there. Kids of any age want love and attention. When they feel valued, they are more likely to follow through.

8. *Ignore unnecessary chatter.* Again, you can't be reacting over everything they say. Pick battles worth fighting and ignore the rest. Some habits get parents all worked up. But kids are kids - they are young and impulsive. For example, you may feel annoyed by the way they tap their foot on the ground when doing something. Correct them, but try to understand why they tap. Are they nervous, anxious, or energized? Try to focus on solving the bigger problems, not just the symptoms.

9. *Be considerate.* If they don't feel like finishing their vegetables today but have been doing so excellently for the past week, give them the

day off. Be a kind and merciful leader. Be flexible so they know that you can be understanding. Your kids need to see that quality in you, or you run the risk of them not confiding in you when they should.

10. *Use the pivot strategy.* Pivot is the art of redirection. Similar to reframing imagination. Pivoting is saying yes instead of no, and still solving the problem. For example, "No, we can't go out before you take a shower". This seems rather negative. Try to rephrase that no into a yes that works for you: "Yes, we will go out - once you have taken your bath". You are saying the same thing, but in a different tone.

Chapter 7: Friendship FAQs

In this final chapter, we tackle some of the most frequently asked questions many parents have when teaching their children social skills and the art of making friends. These questions appear most frequently on social platforms and online parenting forums.

My child doesn't have any friends, should I worry?

We associate friendship with happiness. We think that if our child has lots of friends, it means they are happy. But this isn't always the case. Many kids have a close group of friends and just do fine with them. Some kids only have a single best friend and don't seem to need anyone else. Children all show affection for others in different ways.

It is completely normal for your child to have a few close friends and not an entire army. In fact, the bonds might even be stronger between a select few. But if you are worried that they have no strong friends, then consider your options.

Find out what stands in their way. Are they shy? Do they have specific and unshared interests? Look for the obstacles in their way. As the parent, you know them best, but don't be afraid to ask them.

If they are afraid of rejection, help make some introductions. Or go out of your way to befriend other parents, and bring the children together that way. A dinner party is a small sacrifice to make for the children. But don't force these relationships - they need to develop naturally.

Remind your child that every other child is in the same position. Everyone is scared and nervous, and everyone wants to make a friend. Encourage them to reach out.

Role model the ideal friendships in your own life. Invite your friends around so your children can see these ideas normalized and pick up on patterns of socialization. Be supportive, kind, outgoing, and compassionate towards your friends and hope that your child picks up these values too.

My child is always taken advantage of by their friends. What can I do?

Sometimes life is unfair, and especially to children. The innocents always get hurt the most. As a parent, nothing hurts more than to see a child being treated unfairly and left to suffer alone.

However, as tempting as it seems, you can't be too forceful in ending a bad relationship. Instead, provide guidance, and let them learn from their mistakes. But be ready to catch them when they fall. Consider bringing up in conversation a past friendship in your own life that turned into a toxic relationship. Emphasize how you saw the signs, and how you acted. Be subtle, and turn on your acting charm - but be honest. Again, role model the behaviors you wish your child to adopt.

We have just moved houses and my child doesn't have any friends in this area. How do I encourage him to make new ones?

Introductions are a lot harder in a new place. But be patient. Kids need time to adjust to a new place. This is a lot of information to take in, a lot of anxiety, and they may be hesitant to take on more anxiety in the form of a fragile new friendship.

Just do what you can to keep the options in front of them. Set up playdates or get them involved in school clubs. Invite their study partners over. Even explore the city or neighborhood with them. Give them experiences that make them confident, and confidence will spill over into relationships.

How do I make my child do things without throwing a tantrum or power struggle?

There are certainly days when everything can set a child off. Instead of reacting to their tantrums, act friendly and empathetic. Be their mentor and guide them through their emotions. They must know that you are on their side. Discover what's going on inside - it is almost a guarantee it isn't about whatever "little thing" sets them off (it's never just a little thing).

Just talk to them about it. Be ready to listen. Ask the right questions. Explain your point of view, and why certain tasks need to be completed. Tell them your own feelings - but don't get too heavy. Adults deal with a lot more than a child can handle sometimes.

Simplify your feelings - whether sad, tired, hungry, or sleepy.

This can be an effective way to prevent power struggles because they view you as a concerned parent who genuinely cares and wants to make things better for you. Grow empathy in your household.

Am I in the wrong to fix their problems so they don't feel hurt anymore?

Unfortunately, sometimes you will be in the wrong here. Fixing problems all the time for your child can lead to dependency. Children must be prepared to handle their own problems when they can. You may have the answers, and seeing them go through that negative phase can make your heart ache. But this is how we learn and become self-reliant. Take a single step back - far enough they can discover on their own, but not too far so that you're out of reach.

Encourage wise decision-making with roleplaying. Introduce to them games and activities that improve their cognitive thinking and problem-solving skills. Games like puzzles, riddles, strategy games, and math problems can develop these skills.

My child doesn't share things with me. What should I do?

Many kids, especially teenagers, keep their personal life private. As they grow older, they tend to confide more often in their new social circles, rather than their parents. Depending on your parenting style, they may also be worried about the resulting discipline - or equally important, a lack of discipline, which can be read as a lack of caring.

There are many ways to prevent secrecy, which typically involve growing communication skills. Discuss your daily routines. Be an active listener. Confide in them yourself - but not too much. Remember, adult lives are often too complex for a child to pick up on right now. Emphasize why trust is important, and what dangers lie beyond if that trust is broken. Encourage conversations on subjects that interest them - feign interest if you have to, but always be honest.

Conclusion

Strong friendships are an essential part of a child's life. Friends bring joy and happy expectations about the world. Friends see the best in us and love us for the worst. Friends motivate us to push all limits and set new benchmarks.

Not having such an important figure to rely on early in life can be detrimental. It deprives kids of that joy and love. It prevents them from learning many crucial social skills which are an important asset in life. And importantly, it isolates children with personal problems and no external support system.

This book offered a guide to emphasize the importance of good friends in life, but we also looked at ways that you, as a parent, can play a role. Your role in many cases may simply be to take a step back. It may be to brush up on your own social skills, or take a look at your own actions. Regardless of what actions need to be taken to improve your child's environment, simply acknowledging them is the first step. Weigh your options, and set a course of action.

An important thought we want you to take away from this guide is that it doesn't matter as much if your child is the most popular kid in school, or the one that sits alone at lunch. If your child is happy, then that is something to celebrate. Continue to encourage positive experiences. And if your child is unhappy, then the time for action is now. Remember your guiding role as parent, and be there to listen to whatever your child needs. That's it - that's the core principle. If you can just do that, then you are indeed the best example of being a caring and devoted parent. You've got this.

Thank you for giving this book a read. I hope you loved reading it as much as I enjoyed writing it. It would make me the happiest person on earth if you would take a moment to leave an honest review. All you have to do is visit the site where you purchased this book: It's that simple! The review doesn't have to be a full-fledged paragraph; a few words will do. Your few words will help others decide if this is what they should be reading as well. Thank you in advance, and best of luck with your parenting adventures. Every moment is a joyous one with a child.

References

7 Simple Strategies to Avoid Power Struggles. (2014, October 15).
https://www.psychologytoday.com/intl/blog/what-great-parents-do/201410/7-simple-strategies-avoid-power-struggles

13 Ways to Avoid Power Struggles. (2018, July 17).
https://www.thepathway2success.com/13-ways-to-avoid-power-struggles/

Derhally, L. A. (2016, July 25). The importance of childhood friendships, and how to nurture them.
https://www.washingtonpost.com/news/parenting/wp/2016/07/25/the-importance-of-childhood-friendships-and-how-to-nurture-them/

DeScioli, P., & Kurzban, R. (2009). The alliance hypothesis for human friendship. PLoS ONE.

Dickson, D. J., Huey, M., Laursen, B., Kiuru, N., & Nurmi, J.-E. (2018). Parent contributions to friendship stability during the primary school years. Journal of Family Psychology, 32(2), 217–228.

Essential Friendship Skills for Kids. (n.d.).
https://www.counselorkeri.com/2019/06/17/teach-kids-friendship-skills/

Ferrer, M., & Fugate, A. (n.d.). The Importance of Friendship for School-Age Children. IFAS Extension.

Fletcher, J., Ross, S., & Zhang, Y. (2013). The Consequences of Friendships: Evidence on the Effect of Social Relationships in School on Academic Achievement.

Goldman, J. G. (2013, January 24). How and why do we pick our friends? https://www.bbc.com/future/article/201301 23-what-are-friends-really-for

Improve Skills in Maintaining and Strengthening Friendship Bonds between Kids. (2014, January 1). https://www.lifeway.com/en/articles/parenti ng-family-six-building-blocks-for-friendship

Jones, D. E., Greenberg, M., & Crowley, M. (2015). Early Social-Emotional Functioning and Public Health: The Relationship Between Kindergarten Social Competence and Future Wellness. American Journal of Public Health, 2283_2290.

Lewis, C. S. (1960). The beloved works of C.S. Lewis. New York: HarperCollins Publishers.

McDonald, R., Jouriles, E. N., Ramisetty-Mikler, S., Caetano, R., & Green, C. E. (2006). Estimating the number of American children living in partner-violent families. Journal of Family Psychology, 137-142.

Monnat, S. M., & Chandler, R. F. (2015). Long Term Physical Health Consequences of Adverse Childhood Experiences. The Sociological quarterly, 723–752.

Mourier, J., Vercelloni, J., & Planes, S. (2012). Evidence of social communities in a spatially structured network of a free-ranging shark species. Animal Behaviour, 389-401.

Oakley, J. (2019, September 21). The Risks And Benefits Of Being Your Child's Friend (And Where To Draw The Line). https://www.yourtango.com/2019326645/pa renting-advice-should-friend-your-child

Plato. (2013). Works Of Plato: the trial and death of socrates (Vol. III). New York: Cosimo Classics.

Schwartz, P. (n.d.). Child Behavior: The importance of friendship. https://hvparent.com/importance-of-friendship

Schwarz, N. (2016, February 23). Your Child's
        Friendship Drama: Do's and Don'ts for
        Parents. https://imperfectfamilies.com/your-
        childs-friendship-drama-dos-and-donts-for-
        parents/

Should You Be Your Child's Best Friend? (2019,
        September 19).
        https://kidskingdom.ca/kanata/disciplinaria
        n-or-best-friend-your-role-as-a-parent/

What is a Power Struggle? (2017, February
        27).https://philosophicaltherapist.com/2017
        /02/27/what-is-a-power-struggle/

www.ingramcontent.com/pod-product-compliance
Lightning Source LLC
La Vergne TN
LVHW051428080426
835508LV00022B/3304